This book belongs to

_____

I'm on the way!

WHEN MOMMA LEARNED THAT I WAS ON THE WAY _____

_____

_____

_____

WHAT MOMMA SAID TO DADDY _____

_____

_____

_____

HOW DADDY REACTED _____

_____

_____

_____

I AM EXPECTED TO ARRIVE ON THIS DATE _____

_____

The beginning of my story...

FROM THE ULTRASOUND SCAN IT WAS LEARNED THAT _____

_____

_____

WHILE WAITING FOR ME, MOMMA AND DADDY PICTURED ME AS _____

_____

_____

WHAT MOMMA AND DADDY CALLED ME WHEN I WAS IN HER TUMMY _____

_____

_____

THE HOPES AND DREAMS OF MY PARENTS_____

_____

_____

_____

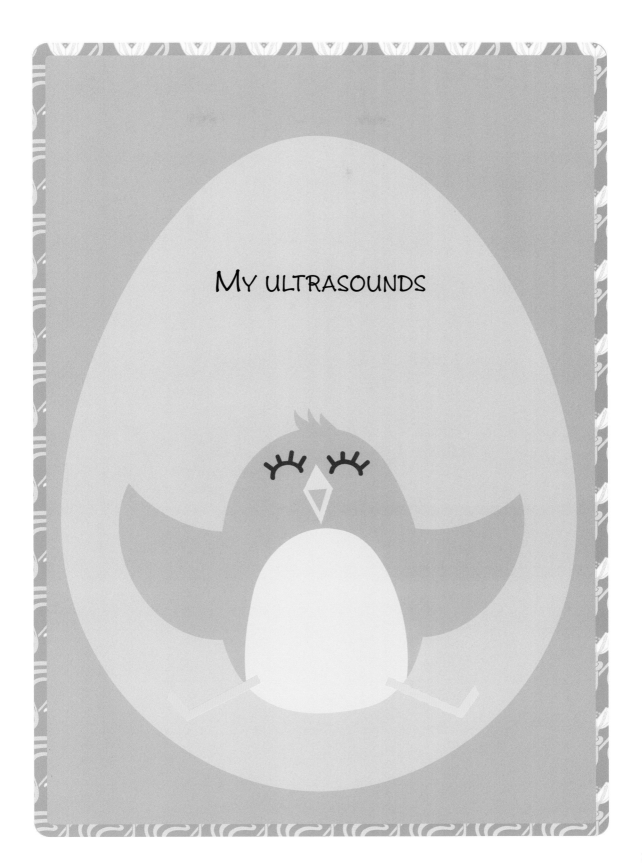

My ultrasounds

My parents

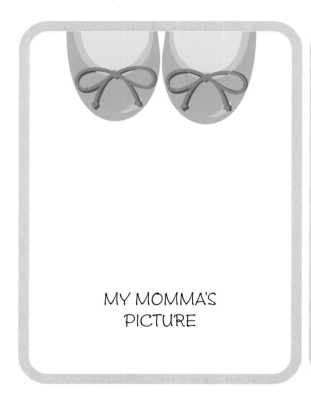

MY MOMMA'S
PICTURE

MY DADDY'S
PICTURE

HOW THEY MET ACCORDING TO MOMMA _____

_____

_____

HOW THEY MET ACCORDING TO DADDY _____

_____

_____

Precious memories

A LOCK OF HAIR

THE HOSPITAL
BRACELET

What they said about me...

MOMMA'S FIRST WORDS _____

_____

_____

_____

DADDY'S FIRST WORDS _____

_____

_____

THE HOPES AND GOOD WISHES OF SIBLINGS, GRANDPARENTS, AUNTS AND

UNCLES, AND FRIENDS _____

_____

_____

_____

_____

WELL WISHERS' CARDS

WELL WISHERS' CARDS I RECEIVED FOR MY BIRTH

MY NAME

_____

My name was chosen by _____

_____

_____

What it means _____

_____

_____

My nickname is _____

_____

My identikit

	At birth
Colour of eyes	
Colour of hair	
Complexion	
Distinguishing features	

AT 6 MONTHS

AT 1 YEAR

MY PHOTOGRAPHS

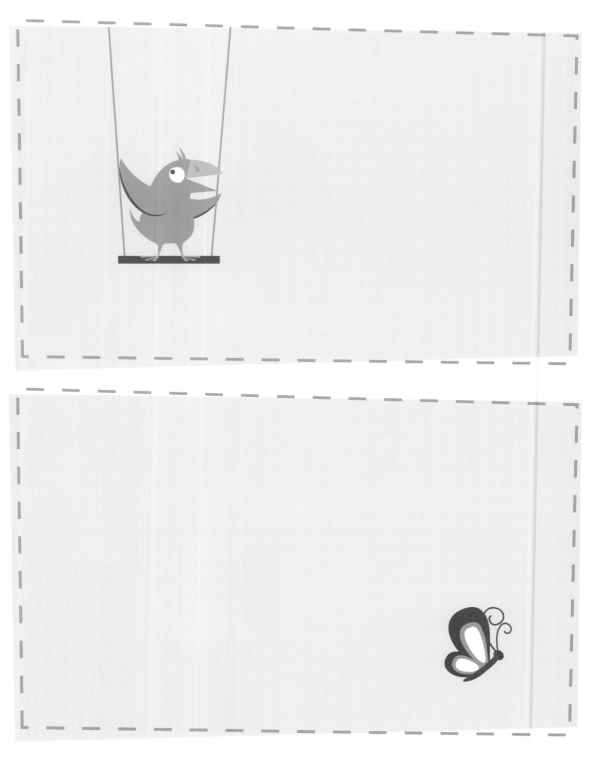

My zodiac sign

ARIES
20 MARCH
20 APRIL

TAURUS
21 APRIL
21 MAY

GEMINI
22 MAY
21 JUNE

CANCER
22 JUNE
22 JULY

LEO
23 JULY
22 AUGUST

VIRGO
23 AUGUST
22 SEPTEMBER

MY ZODIAC SIGN IS

LIBRA

23 SEPTEMBER
22 OCTOBER

SCORPIO

23 OCTOBER
22 NOVEMBER

SAGITTARIUS

23 NOVEMBER
21 DECEMBER

CAPRICORN

22 DECEMBER
20 JANUARY

AQUARIUS

21 JANUARY
19 FEBRUARY

PISCES

20 FEBRUARY
19 MARCH

THE CHARACTERISTICS OF THIS SIGN ARE _____

THE MAIN EVENTS OF THE PERIOD _____

_____

_____

THE HIT SONGS _____

_____

THE MOST POPULAR MOVIES _____

_____

_____

THE BEST-SELLING BOOKS _____

_____

_____

THE WORLD LEADERS ARE _____

_____

SOME CURRENT PRICES _____

_____

_____

HAIR _____

_____

EARS _____

_____

DISTINGUISHING FEATURES _____

_____

My family tree

MOMMY

Welcome home !

MY FIRTS ADDRESS _____

_____

_____

_____

ON THE RIDE HOME _____

_____

_____

_____

WHO WAS WAITING FOR ME _____

_____

_____

_____

MY BEDROOM _____

_____

_____

About the doctor

My pediatrician _____

_____

The first time I went to the doctor _____

_____

_____

My blood type _____

Vaccinations _____

_____

_____

_____

My first illnesses _____

_____

_____

_____

My foot print

Wake up, sleepyhead!

How I announce that I'm awake _____

_____

_____

_____

_____

_____

_____

My waking up habits _____

_____

_____

_____

The bath is ready

My first time in the bath _____

_____

_____

_____

How I reacted _____

_____

_____

_____

In the bath I play with _____

_____

_____

_____

My food is ready

My first solid food _____

_____

_____

Momma's recipes _____

_____

_____

_____

_____

_____

MY FAVORITE FOOD _____

_____

_____

_____

_____

I DON'T LIKE _____

_____

_____

_____

_____

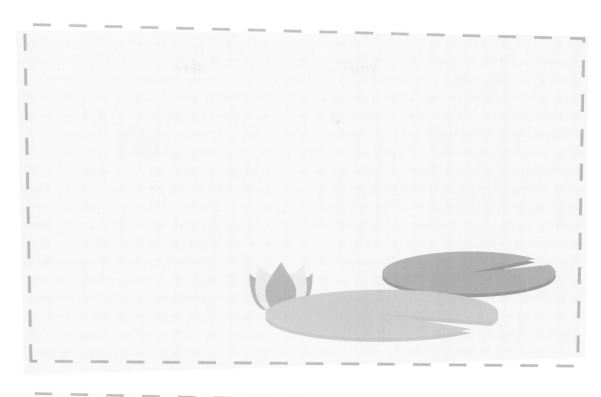

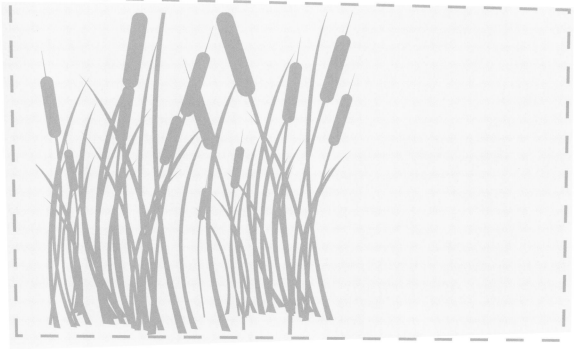

Golden dreams

My first night _____

_____

_____

_____

_____

MY FIRST WHOLE NIGHT'S SLEEP _____

_____

_____

_____

_____

_____

_____

_____

_____

_____

To go to sleep I need...

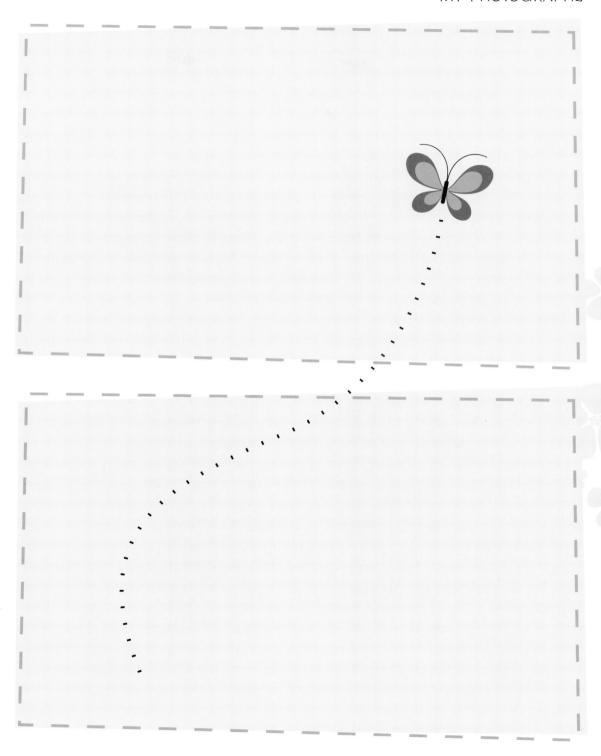

My day

AT ONE MONTH

SLEEPING TIMES _____

_____

FEEDING TIMES _____

_____

PLAY TIMES _____

_____

AT THREE MONTHS

SLEEPING TIMES _____

_____

FEEDING TIMES _____

_____

PLAY TIMES _____

_____

AT SIX MONTHS

Sleeping times _____

_____

Feeding times _____

_____

Play times _____

_____

AT NINE MONTHS

Sleeping times _____

_____

Feeding times _____

_____

Play times _____

_____

AT TWELVE MONTHS

Sleeping times _____

_____

Feeding times _____

_____

Play times _____

_____

Mummy's memories _____

_____

_____

_____

_____

My first appearance in public

OUR FAMILY'S FIRST WALK TOOK PLACE

_____

_____

_____

_____

_____

HOW I REACTED

_____

_____

_____

_____

_____

_____

THE PEOPLE I MET SAID TO ME _____

_____

_____

_____

_____

MY FAVORITE PLACES ARE _____

_____

_____

_____

MY PHOTOGRAPHS

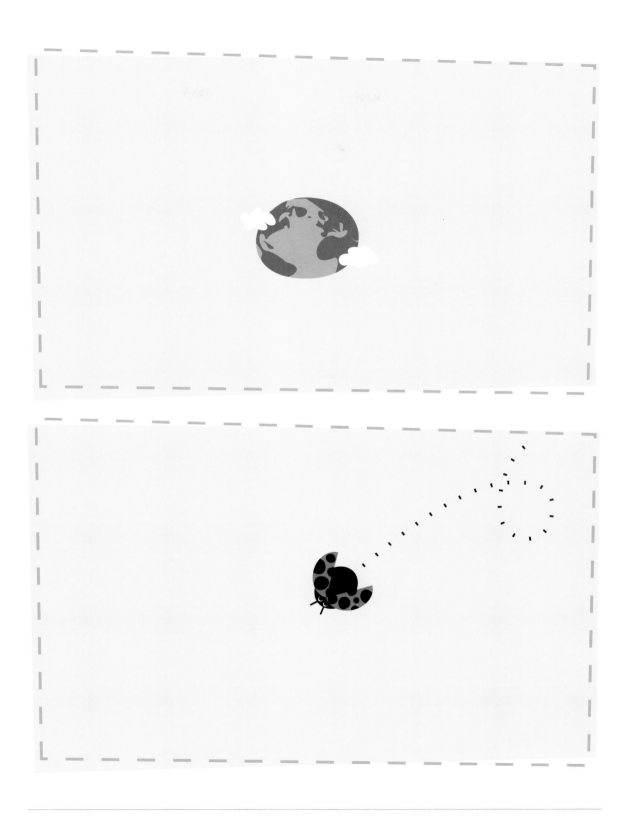

A world to explore

THE FIRST TIME THAT:

I WENT IN AN AUTOMOBILE _____

_____

_____

I WENT ON A TRAIN, AN AIRPLANE OR A SHIP _____

_____

_____

_____

_____

_____

I WENT ON HOLIDAY WITH MY FAMILY _____

_____

_____

I SAW THE SEA _____

_____

_____

I FELT THE SNOW _____

_____

_____

_____

MY PHOTOGRAPHS

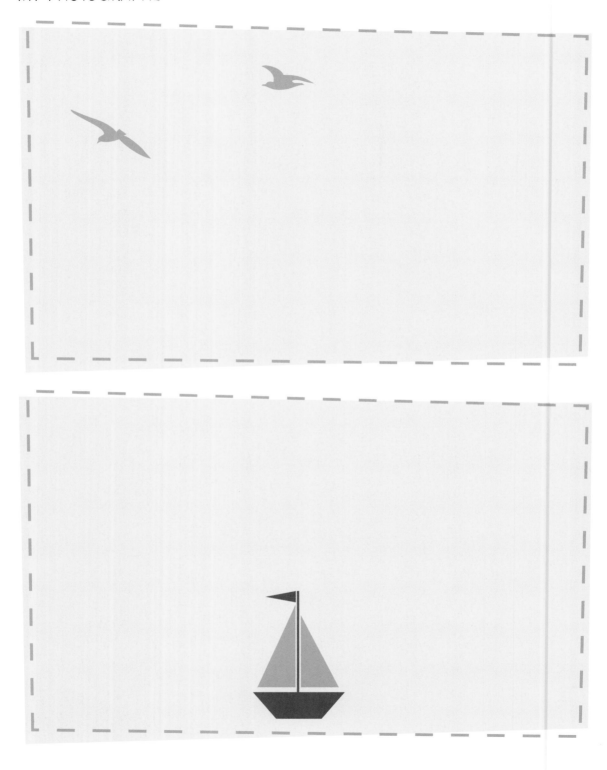

I MADE MY FIRST STEPS WITH A LITTLE HELP

_____

_____

_____

I WALKED ON MY OWN FOR THE FIRST TIME _____

_____

_____

I STARTED DANCING _____

_____

_____

I RAN ON AHEAD ON MY OWN! _____

_____

_____

_____

What's my mood

THINGS THAT MAKE ME HAPPY

_____

_____

_____

_____

_____

_____

THINGS THAT MAKE ME LAUGH

_____

_____

_____

_____

_____

_____

THINGS THAT MAKE ME ANGRY

WHAT COMFORTS ME

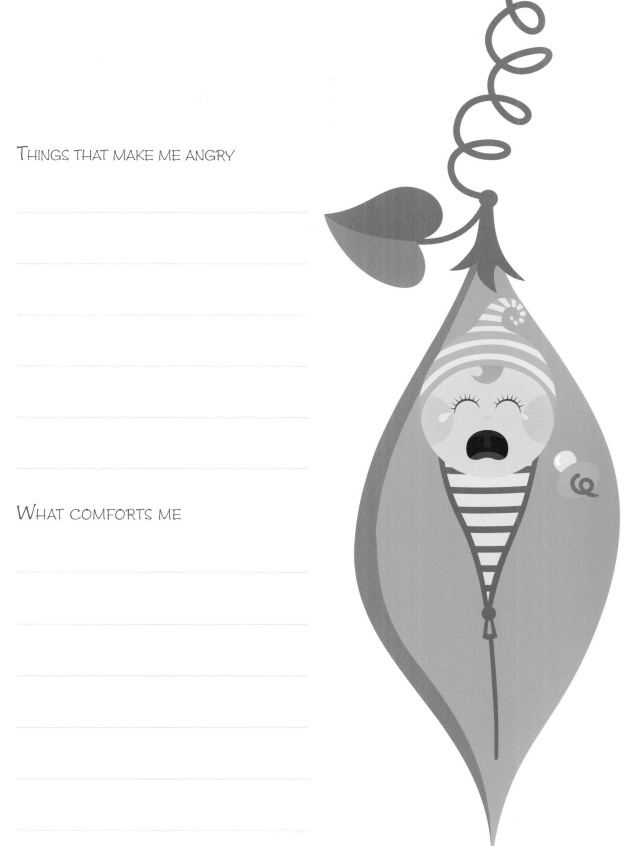

My favorites

COLORS _____

_____

FAIRY TALE CHARACTERS _____

_____

CLOTHES _____

_____

ROOMS _____

_____

CARTOONS _____

_____

TOYS _____

_____

GAMES _____

_____

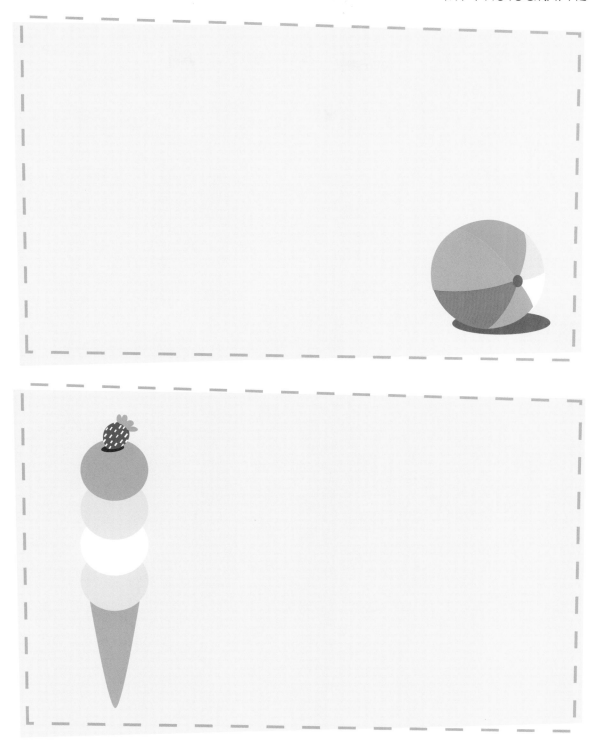

A special day

Event _____

_____

_____

Who was there _____

_____

_____

_____

An unforgettable memory _____

_____

_____

_____

My first birthday

When and where the party took place _____

_____

_____

The guests _____

_____

_____

My "look" for the occasion _____

_____

Gifts received _____

_____

I remember that _____

_____

_____

MY PHOTOGRAPHS

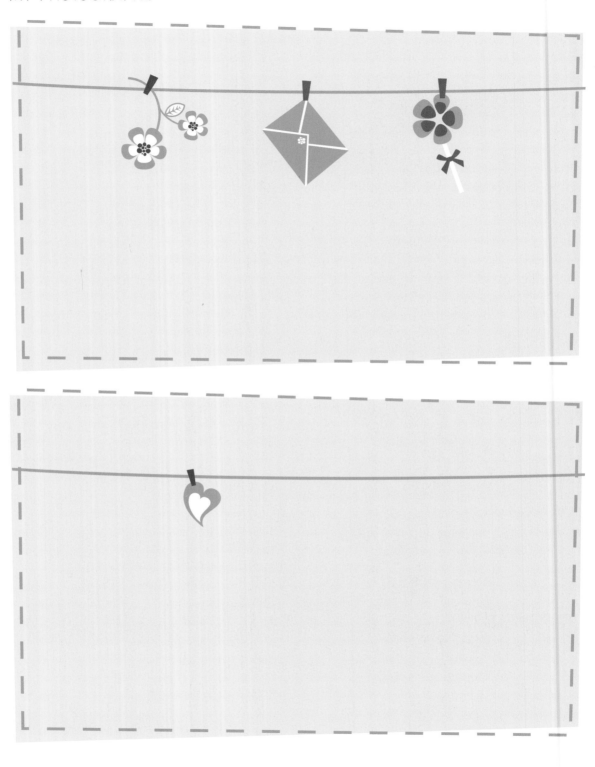

IN THE LAST 12 MONTHS MOMMA AND DADDY HAVE NEVER FORGOTTEN

THE TIME WHEN I... _____

_____

_____

_____

WHAT I LEARNED TO DO THIS YEAR _____

_____

_____

_____

MY PERSONALITY _____

_____

_____

_____

HOW MUCH I HAVE GROWN IN ONE YEAR

WEIGHT _____ HEIGHT _____

My favorites!

Fairy tale _____

Song _____

Toy _____

Cartoon _____

Stuffed animal _____

Game _____

Garment _____

The thing that makes me happiest

_____

_____

The thing that makes me upset

_____

_____

The thing that comforts me

_____

_____

There is always a first time

I BUILT A TOWER _____

_____

I TRIED TO GET DRESSED ON MY OWN _____

_____

I ATE ON MY OWN _____

_____

I THREW A BALL IN THE AIR _____

_____

I JUMPED _____

_____

MY NEW EXPERIENCES _____

_____

_____

_____

Famous
first words

THE FIRST WORD I SPOKE WAS _____

_____

_____

HOW I PRONOUNCED IT _____

_____

_____

_____

_____

I SAID "MOMMA" FOR THE FIRST TIME _____

_____

_____

_____

I SAID "DADDY" FOR THE FIRST TIME _____

_____

_____

_____

A special day

EVENT _____

_____

WHO WAS THERE _____

_____

_____

_____

_____

AN UNFORGETTABLE MEMORY _____

_____

_____

_____

_____

Traveling!

OUR DESTINATION _____

_____

_____

SOMETHING WE SAW _____

_____

_____

HOW I BEHAVED _____

_____

_____

A SPECIAL MEMORY _____

_____

_____

_____

MY PHOTOGRAPHS

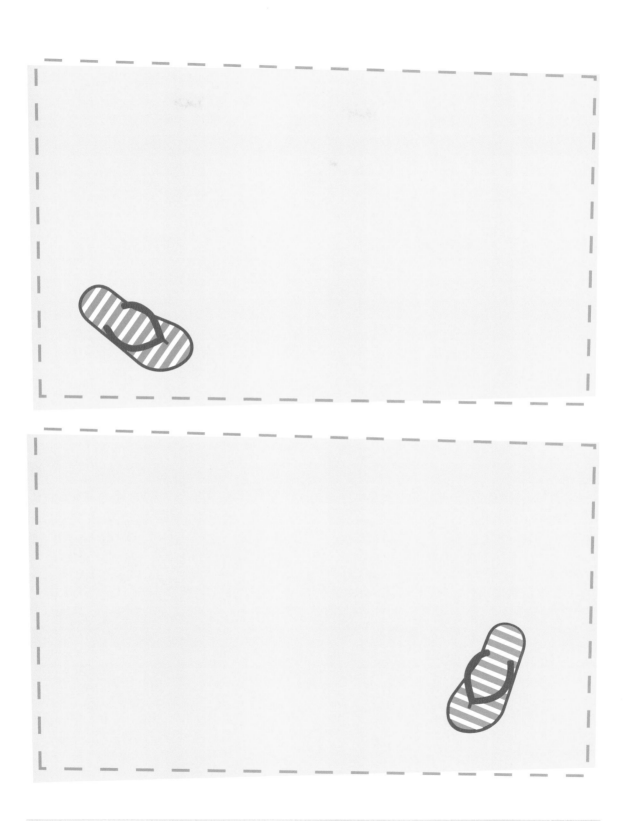

My second birthday

WHEN AND WHERE THE PARTY TOOK PLACE _____

_____

MY "LOOK" FOR THE OCCASION _____

_____

_____

GIFTS RECEIVED _____

_____

_____

I REMEMBER THAT_____

_____

_____

_____

THE GUESTS

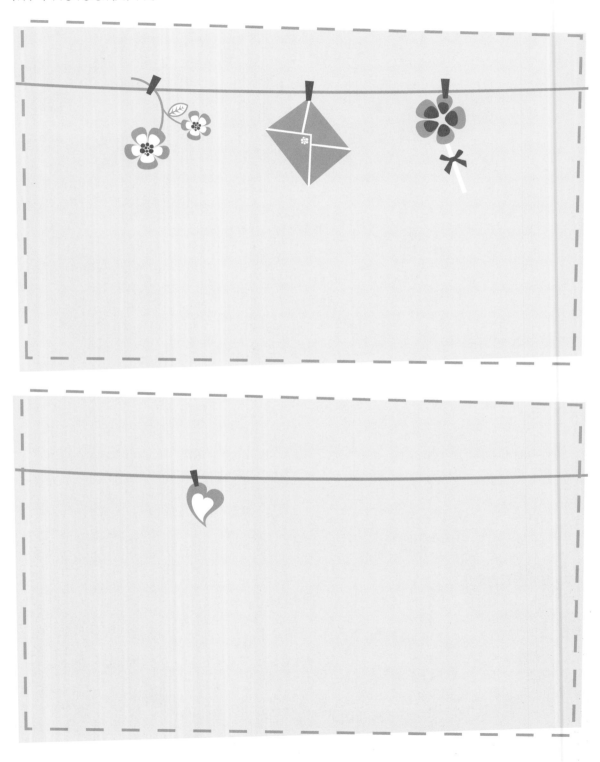

IN THE LAST 12 MONTHS MOMMA AND DADDY HAVE NEVER FORGOTTEN

THE TIME WHEN I... _____

_____

_____

_____

WHAT I LEARNED TO DO THIS YEAR _____

_____

_____

_____

MY PERSONALITY _____

_____

_____

_____

HOW MUCH I HAVE GROWN IN ONE YEAR

WEIGHT _____ HEIGHT _____

Fairy tale _____

Song _____

Toy _____

Cartoon _____

Stuffed animal _____

Game _____

_____

Garment _____

The thing that makes me happiest _____

_____

The thing that makes me upset _____

_____

The thing that comforts me _____

_____

_____

There is always a first time

I STOPPED WEARING DIAPERS _____

I DREW A CIRCLE _____

I RECOGNIZED COLORS _____

I COUNTED UP TO FIVE _____

I BRUSHED MY TEETH MYSELF _____

I RODE A TRYCICLE _____

I DRESSED ON MY OWN _____

I USED MY OWN NAME _____

A NEW EXPERIENCE _____

_____

_____

_____

_____

A special day

EVENT _____

_____

WHO WAS THERE _____

_____

_____

_____

_____

_____

AN UNFORGETTABLE MEMORY _____

_____

_____

_____

_____

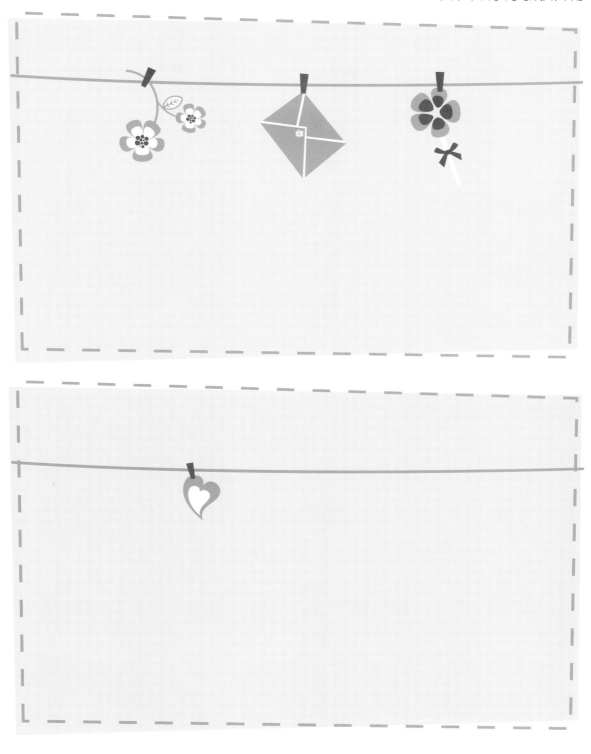

Traveling!

OUR DESTINATION _____

_____

SOMETHING WE SAW _____

_____

_____

_____

_____

HOW I BEHAVED _____

_____

_____

_____

A SPECIAL MEMORY _____

_____

_____

_____

MY PHOTOGRAPHS

My third birthday!

WHEN AND WHERE THE PARTY TOOK PLACE _____

_____

THE GUESTS _____

_____

_____

MY "LOOK" FOR THE OCCASION _____

_____

GIFTS RECEIVED _____

_____

_____

I REMEMBER THAT _____

_____

_____

_____

MY PHOTOGRAPHS

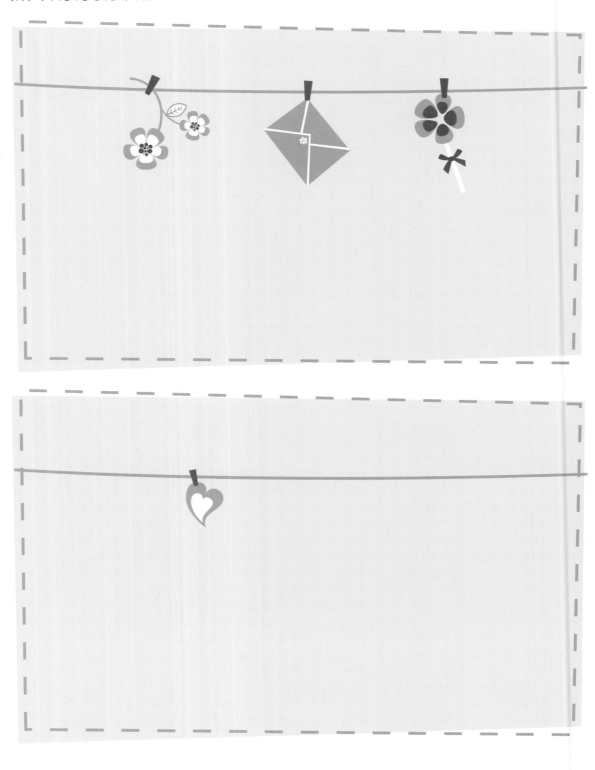

IN THE LAST 12 MONTHS MOMMA AND DADDY HAVE NEVER FORGOTTEN

THE TIME WHEN I... _____

_____

_____

_____

WHAT I LEARNED TO DO THIS YEAR _____

_____

_____

_____

MY PERSONALITY _____

_____

_____

_____

HOW MUCH I HAVE GROWN IN ONE YEAR

WEIGHT _____ HEIGHT _____

My favorites!

FAIRY TALE _____

SONG _____

TOY _____

CARTOON _____

STUFFED ANIMAL _____

GAME _____

GARMENT _____

THE THING THAT MAKES ME HAPPIEST _____

_____

THE THING THAT MAKES ME UPSET _____

_____

THE THING THAT COMFORTS ME _____

_____

There is always a first time

I DREW A PICTURE OF AN ANIMAL _____

_____

_____

I WENT TO A FRIEND'S PARTY _____

_____

_____

I CHOSE MY CLOTHES IN THE MORNING _____

_____

_____

I WROTE MY OWN NAME _____

_____

_____

I STOPPED USING A PACIFIER _____

_____

My first time at preschool

The teacher

My favorite games

My reactions

Friends...

My new friends are called _____

_____

_____

_____

With them I play these games _____

_____

_____

My best friend is

_____

My best friend's birthday is

_____

With my best friend I play _____

_____

_____

Traveling!

Our destination _____

_____

_____

Something we saw _____

_____

_____

How I behaved _____

_____

_____

A special memory _____

_____

_____

_____